Low Light Photography

Book 3
in
Quick Tips from a
Pro Photographer
Series

by Julia Harwood

Table of Contents

1. Low Light Photography Introduction

Low light photography - the first thing you need for low light photography, apart from your camera, is a tripod, low light photography involves long shutter speeds and so we need to stabilise our camera.

A note here, with modern cameras able to handle high ISO much better, we think we can just increase the ISO and hand hold the camera, but a lot of the effects that are created using long exposures will be lost, for example, light trails, silky water, multiple fireworks etc.

When using a tripod there are a few things to remember, first make sure it is on a stable surface and that there are not a lot of vibrations or strong winds, if there are strong winds, be sure to anchor your tripod with weights, or attach your camera bag to it to act as a weight. You can also get vibration suppressing feet for your tripod.

Next we need to turn image stabilisation off. One of the quirks of image stabilisation (IS) is that if there is absolutely no movement it creates movement. Camera manufacturers are recognising this and some cameras now have a tripod mode in the IS menu, so if you have this option use it. I recommend putting a sticker on the top of your tripod saying is IS off.

This reminds you to turn it off and jogs your memory to turn it back on when you take it off the tripod. Remember to turn the IS off on the lens too if it has it.

The other thing we need to look out for is movement caused by mirror slap, in non DSLR or mirrorless cameras we don't need to worry about this, but in DSLR's we do. You can check your manual to see how to lock the mirror, but most cameras lock the mirror when in live mode, so go to live mode before taking the shot.

This brings us to the next thing we need, a shutter release, these come in corded varieties and wireless varieties.

If you don't have one then you can improvise with the timer function on your camera, try it at 2 sec, if you still have camera shake then use 10 sec. Also get in the habit of rolling your finger off the shutter button rather than pressing and lifting off.

Often night photos will have more noise in them than we want, this can be from a high ISO or from long shutter speeds. A way to fix this is to take a black frame or dark frame image. When you have taken a shot, then put your lens cap on and cover the viewfinder as well, some camera straps have a piece that will fit in the viewfinder for this or devise your own little hood, and take a shot keeping exactly the same exposure that you just used for the image.

When you are processing the image, add original image to your post processing program and then add the black frame image, select this image and copy it, then go to the original image and paste this black frame image into it. Now set the blend mode to subtract or difference and move the opacity until you get the best effect. If you didn't do the dark frame at the time all is not lost, there is an app called HotPixels Eliminator have a look here for more information http://www.mediachance.com/digicam/hotpixels.htm

So now we are set-up let's look at different types of low light photography.

2. Sunsets and Sunrises

These are a favorite as they are often readily available and everyone loves a great sunrise and sunset. These require only a slightly slow shutter speed and a lot of cameras have settings specifically for them, but they raise the ISO which means the image is not as sharp and you may get a noisy image, if you don't have a tripod this is a great fall back option.

Use your spot exposure and expose on the brightest part of the image, this will really bring out the colors in the sky.

You can even do this on your phone, point your camera at the sunset and touch your screen at the brightest point, now take the shot and you will have much more vibrant images.

If using manual settings play with bracketing your shots to 0, -1, and -2. Often the darker the image the more vibrant the colors, but be careful not to have a solid black foreground unless you are going for a silhouette.

If there are reflections of the sunset, for example in water then put your horizon in the center, otherwise place it on the lower third of the image so we see the most of the sky.

Speaking of water, if there is water in the image, try adding a Neutral Density (ND) filter to make a longer exposure and create the silky smooth water.

If you don't have an ND filter then use a polarising filter, it removes glare and intensifies colors.

Two final tips for sunset/sunrise photography, firstly turn around and look behind you, often the sky opposite the sunrise/sunset is just as dramatic as the way we normally look and finally for sunrise get there half an hour before and for sunset stay half an hour after, this is often when we get the most drama in the sky.

Often I have thought it's all over and everyone has left and I wait for 20 minutes and the sky turns to red and an amazing sky-show happens for 10 minutes and then is all over. Allow time to just sit and enjoy or relax as you wait for the pre or post show.

A final note here, if you are at the beach taking sunset/sunrise, choose the lens you want before you go and stick with it, sand is deadly to sensors and if you change lenses on the beach you are highly likely to get sand in the camera.

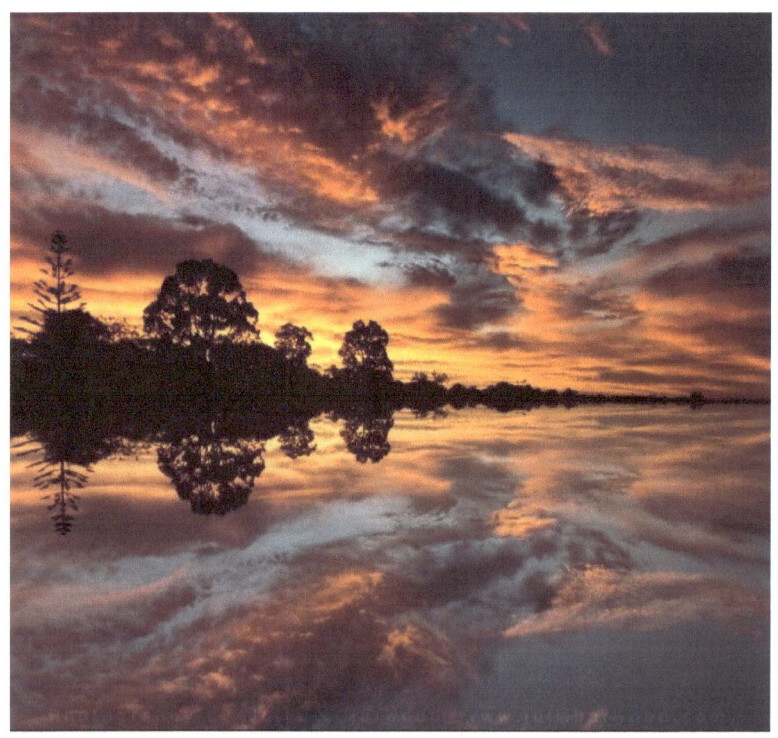

3. Fireworks

This is another slow shutter speed situation. Usually I set the camera to 2 seconds and then fire away. You can experiment with 2-3 sec. If you get too many fireworks in the one shot then you lose the effect as the image just becomes white light due to the brightness of the fireworks.

Always turn your camera to portrait orientation and shoot with a wide angle lens so that you get the low and the high fireworks. Usually you will just focus on infinity and use F8, if there is illuminated foreground you want to capture use f11 and focus just past the foreground to get it in focus as well as the fireworks. This works if there are reflections in the water too.

Fireworks are very easy to combine in post processing, so if you don't have all the right gear with you then test out the scene mode for fireworks.

Again, see the top section on tripod and cable release, as you want to use these if you can.

Once you have taken the shots and loaded them onto the computer, open up your post processing software and if you have a levels adjustment, open this and click the black eyedropper on parts of the sky until it is all black, this really finishes off your fireworks images.

When you combine images of fireworks set the blend mode on the background layer to normal and then each layer you add change the blend mode to Linear Dodge and they will blend seamlessly.

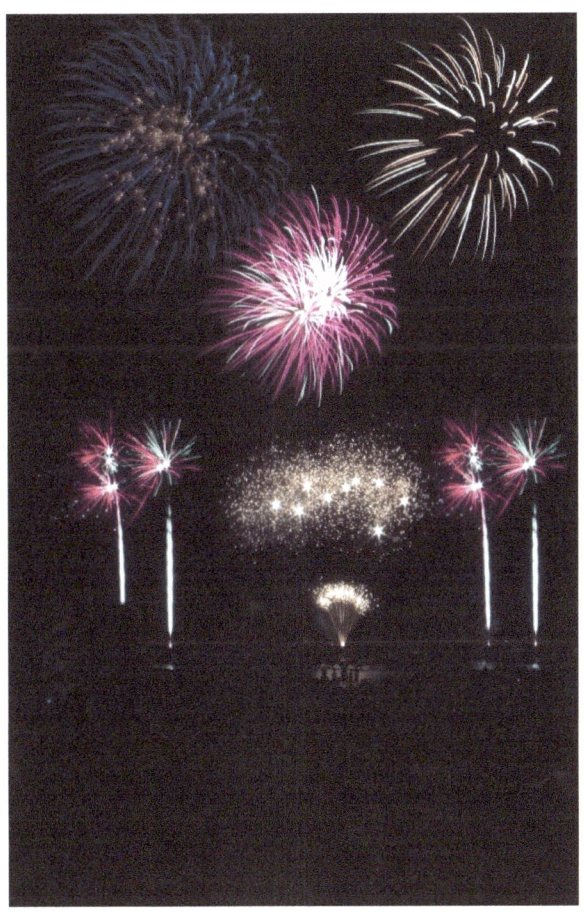

4. Water

Water is one subject that a lot of people want to take photograph, with low light photography or slow shutter speeds we get the beautiful silky water you see in pictures and go, "wow, that is amazing".

It really does add the "Wow" factor, whether to a waterfall, a stream or a seascape. So How do we do it?

Firstly we need to create low light, even shooting seascapes at dusk or dawn often won't create the effects you want as there is a trick to getting a slow enough shutter speed.

You can do it by using a Neutral Density Filter or ND filter. These come in different strengths, from 1 to 10 and you can even get a variable one which covers all the bases which is what I use. They cost more but keep your kit light and you have whatever you need for any situation without having to change filters all the time.

Obviously as this is low light photography you will need a tripod and a shutter release or use the timer function on the camera. Remember to turn IS off and use live view to lock your mirror up, now you are ready to go. Go find some water and start playing.

You will usually want a large depth of field which is great as this lets in the least amount of light, so go to your highest f stop and then come back one. Why come back one?

Cameras often preform better in the mid ranges compared to the extremities so if we come back one we should get a better image.

The same applies to focal length, if you are shooting wide angle and you have a zoom then go to the widest and then come back in a bit. Remember for waterfalls you can turn the cameras orientation to portrait.

The shutter speed you will want is as low as possible, so experiment, start from the lowest you can get and if that is too silky then increase the shutter speed until you get what you like.

ISO should be set to 100.

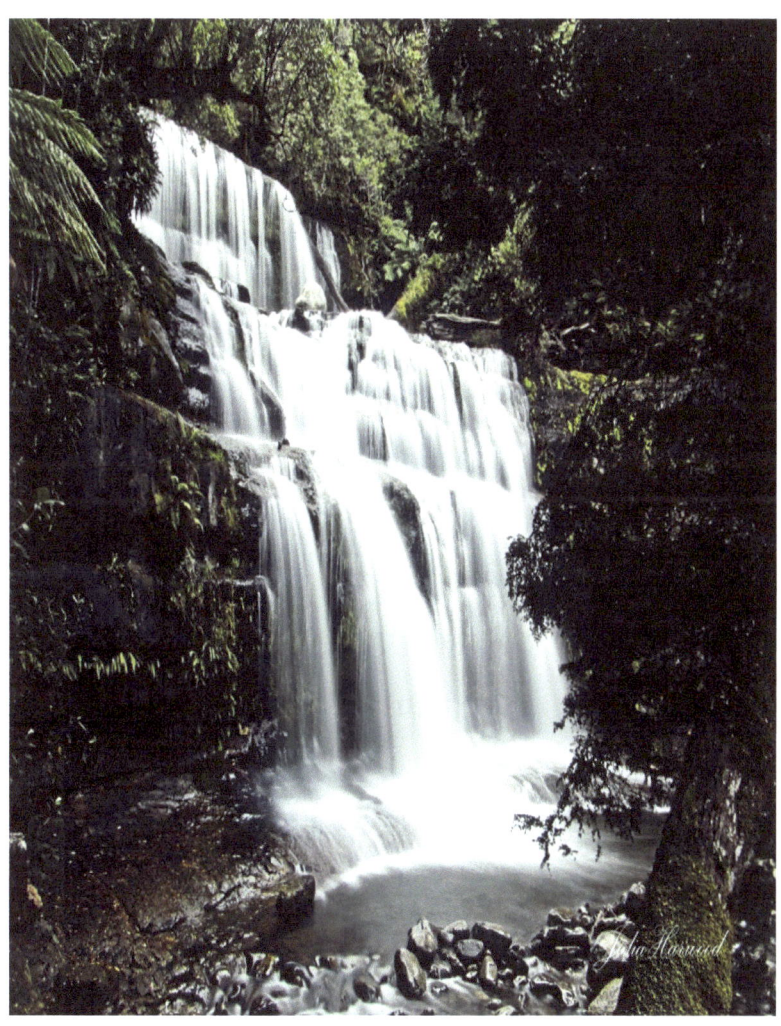

5. Light Trails

These are captured when we have moving vehicles in an image when we are using a slow shutter speed. You would normally do this at night, but if you use an ND filter you can try it out at different times.

You will need your tripod and a shutter release or use the timer function on the camera. Remember to turn IS off and use live view to lock your mirror up.

Start with the following settings:

ISO 100
Shutter speed 5sec
Aperture whatever is needed to get this shutter speed.

A note here, we only need control of the shutter speed on this one so we can use the "S" mode or Shutter priority mode and set this to 5 sec and the camera will set the aperture, but make sure your ISO is 100.

We set the ISO to 100 to get a longer shutter speed and to decrease the noise. We will get some noise in long shutter speed photography so we don't want to add any extra.

Bridges are great places for these as the traffic comes right under you, but you often get vibration on bridges, so make sure you have something to hang on your tripod to stop movement, your camera bag works well for this. Vibration dampening feet on your tripod will help too.

6. Night Scenes

These are an easy one in that you can get them anywhere, however the best time for these is during the blue hour. Blue hour is usually only about 20mins after the sun has set and before the sky goes full black. This gives you some light so you don't generally need as long a shutter speed which in turn means you can get the scene nicely lit without blowing out any lights in the scene.

If you wait till later then you will need a really long shutter speed to capture the scene and with a long shutter speed the lights will become too bright.

If you don't have a choice and it is already full black then use a torch to paint over the areas that are most important to the scene or just to wash over the whole area. Most people have a torch on their phones and you can get apps that give you different colored light and stronger light.

A note on safety here, take a friend with you so that you are not out alone after dark. We get so engrossed in what we are doing we are not as vigilant as we might otherwise be and you are carrying some expensive gear, so have a friend so they can lookout for you and warn of any impending danger. There is also safety in numbers and remember it is always Safety first.

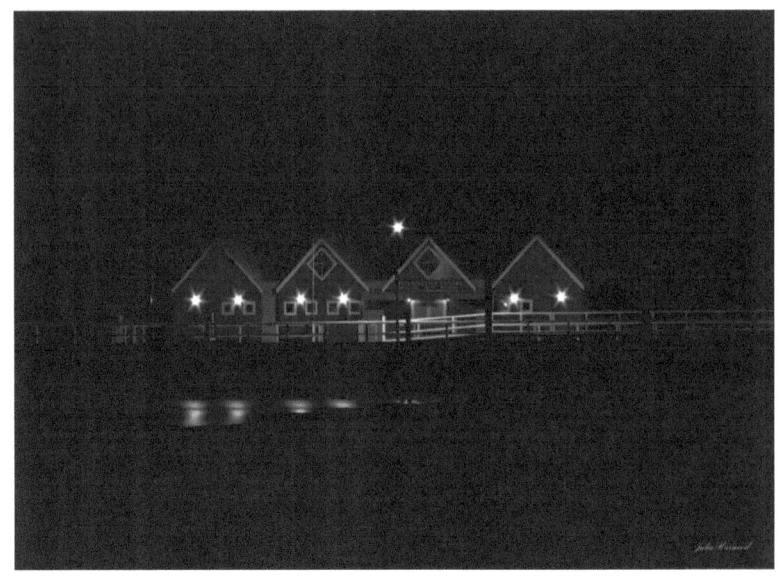

7. Star Trails

Now these we take later in the night. To get nice star trails you really need to get away from the light that civilisation generates and out in the country where you are away from any light sources.

These are really long shutter speeds, so you will need a shutter release that locks. Otherwise you have to sit holding the button for hours. You can do these in one sitting, using as long as your battery will allow, make sure you don't run the battery flat before it has finished processing the image.

The other way you can do it is in 30 sec sequences and then stitch them together in Photoshop or a similar post processing software program.

Stars are a really long way away so you can focus on infinity and set your aperture to f8 or there about. You will probably need to start with an ISO of 3200 to get the stars showing clearly and not moving. This will give you a clear shot of the stars, gradually decrease the ISO until you still get the stars but they are leaving trails.

To focus on infinity, manually set your focus or shine a light on something a fair way away, then set the focus lock using the AF lock button on the back of your camera. If you don't know where it is or how it works then read your manual. You can also use your manual focus and focus to infinity.

This type of photography is a lot of trial and error as no two nights have the same light, so allow yourself plenty of time to play.

These images often look best with some form of a scene silhouetted, or some areas light up with a torch, but try to pick one with non moving subjects, such as rocks or structures as trees will show movement in the branches. If it is a still night this will probably be fine, but if not you may just end up with a blur.

8. Light Painting

This is a lot of fun. Again best done in the blue hour and on a night with a full moon if you want to include the scene. You will need a tripod and a shutter release or timer function. Set your camera and tripod up so that you can see the scene, use as wide an angle as your lens allows.

Remember to wear dark clothing so you won't show up in the shot.

You will also need a light source; it can be your phone, a torch, a glow stick or steel wool that you set on fire. (You need to have this attached to something, most people use a kitchen whisk but make sure you have something around the handle so it doesn't get hot and burn you.

Also be aware that the Sparks can start fires, so only do this where there is nothing that can catch fire and that there is not a total fire ban.)

As you move the light source around it will leave trails, because you are moving and in dark clothes the camera won't see you.

To create an orb you attach your light to a string and twirl it around you, if you keep turning as you do this you will achieve an orb.

You can write with light but you need to write backwards. This is fun to do at the beach as you can write backwards in the sand and then it is easier to do.

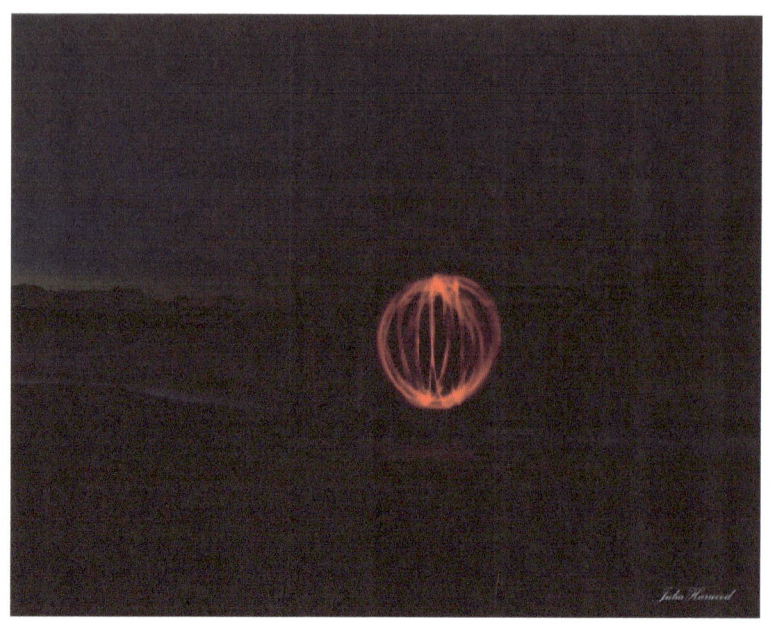

9. Ghosts and Campfires

When we use a slow shutter speed and people move around they become ghosts if they move quick enough or if we have a long enough shutter speed they won't even appear in the image, so you can have a lot of fun adding ghosts to an image.

Campfires or bonfires can be tricky as the light source is so intense. You need to expose so the brightest areas are not over exposed, then if you add a fill flash you will get some of the scene and people around the fire. Again this is often trial and error to get the settings right.

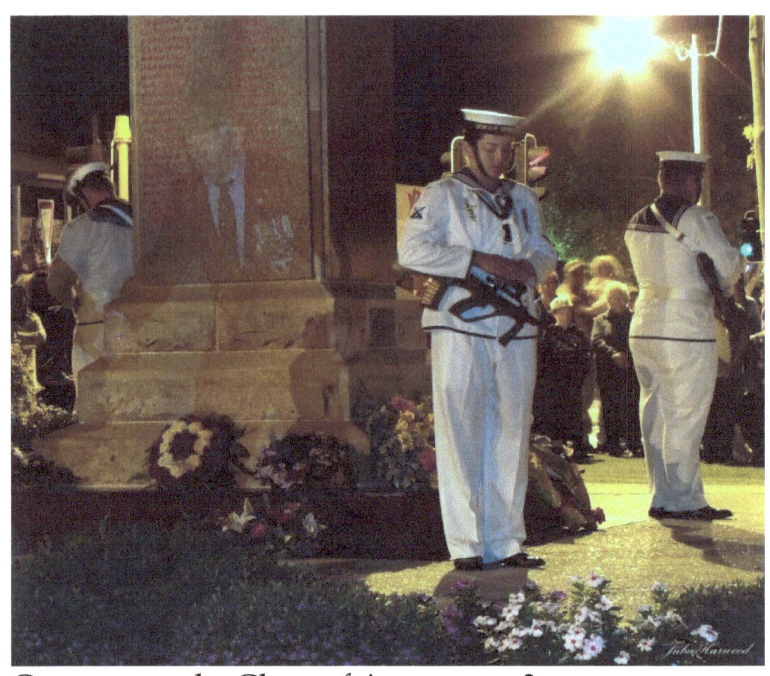

Can you see the Ghost of Anzacs past?

10. Moon

The moon is actually quite easy to capture, especially the full moon as it is a bright light source in itself, however you do need a long lens to capture it large. You will find when you set your exposure that the moon will be just a bright spot, but if you keep increasing the shutter speed or decreasing your ISO you will get to the point where it is just right.

Start with ISO 100, f8 and then set the shutter speed according to the camera light meter. This is the line in the camera which has a notch in the middle, we want to be as close to this middle notch to have a well exposed image. Start here, but then keep on easing the shutter speed until you get the look you want.

Remember the moon is moving so if you use a long exposure you will get movement.

Additional Reading
http://photo.stackexchange.com/questions/459/how-do-i-set-the-proper-exposure-for-nighttime-moon-photos

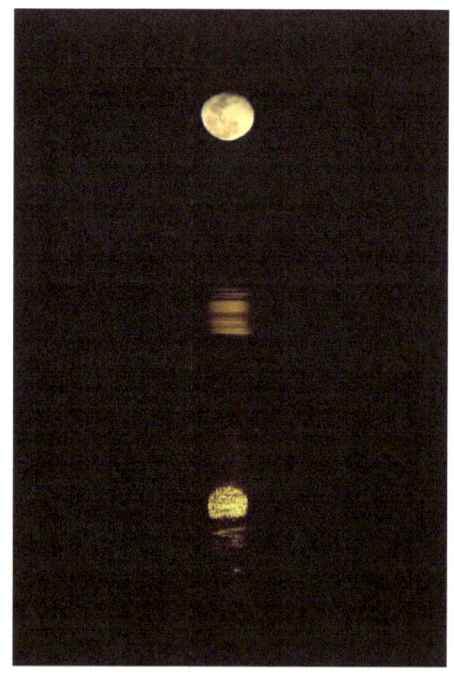

11. Lightening

You can buy lightening triggers that automatically take the shot when lightening strikes, but if lightening starts and you don't have this, set your shutter speed to 1/60 if you are hand holding the camera and set the camera to burst mode. Focus on infinity and use an f stop of around f5.6 and as soon as you glimpse lightening hold the shutter button down. This is very hit and miss but will give you a good chance if you don't have a lightening trigger. Obviously the more lightening flashes the easier it is to get some. Remember safety first, don't put yourself anywhere where you are likely to get hit by lightening and make sure your camera is protected from the rain.

Additional reading
Night exposure guide
http://media.digitalcameraworld.com/wp-content/uploads/sites/123/2012/11/Night_photography_exposure_guide_photography_cheat_sheet.jpg

These are quick tips, so not designed to go into great detail, if you want to know more there is a Photographic Course I recommend called the PhotoDash and you can find out more here. http://www.digital-photo-secrets.com/thedash/
They have different topics each month, so keep a look out for the low light photography topics.

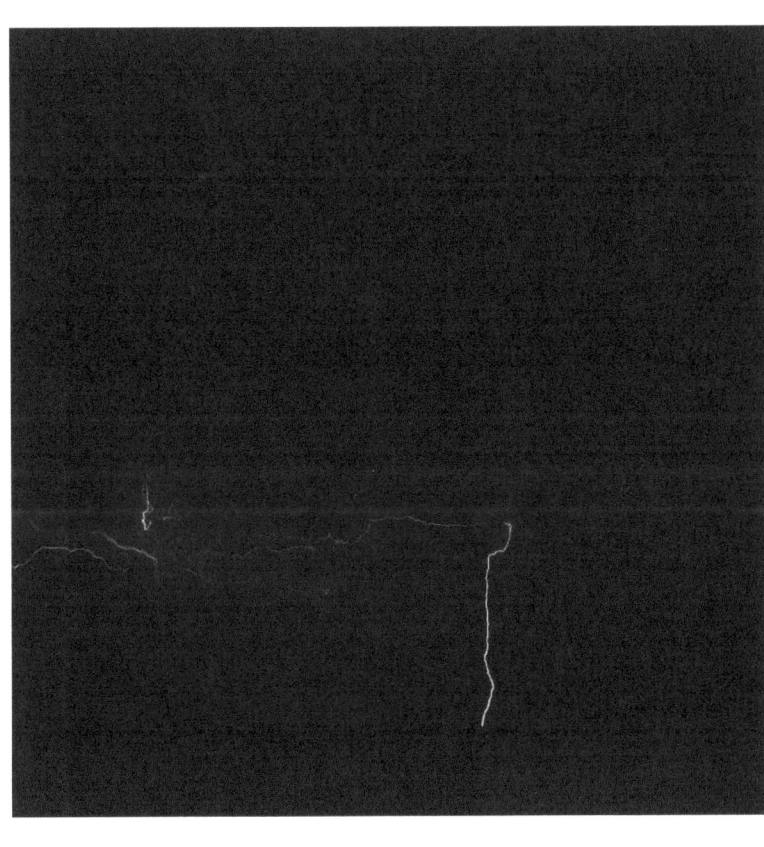

12. Cheat Sheet - Low Light Photography

Low Light Photography
Tripod
IS (image stabilization) OFF
Shutter release or timer
Live View (for DSLRs)
Torch or head light (red light is best)
Dark clothing if light painting
ND filter
Polarising filter

Fireworks
 Shutter speed 2-3 seconds
Aperture f5.6 – f 8
ISO100
Wide angle lens
Portrait orientation
Timer function or remote release
Manual focus before full dark and leave it here

Sunrise/sunset
Aperture f11 or higher
Shutter speed set to correct exposure
then bracket -1 and -2
ISO100
Polariser or ND filter
Look behind you
Stay for 20mins afterwards
Focus 1/3 of the way into scene

Waterfalls
ISO 100
Aperture F8 upward
Shutter speed, get it as low as you can
while still having a correct exposure.
Focus a third of way in to scene if getting whole
scene
If just waterfall, focus on waterfall.

Light Trails
ISO 100
Shutter speed 5sec
Aperture f8
Focus on start of lights

Night Scenes
Blue hour
ISO100
Aperture f5.6 or higher
Shutter speed, whatever is needed for a correct exposure
Focus a third of way into scene

Stars - stationary
ISO3200
Aperture f8
Shutter speed, whatever is needed to get correct exposure
Focus on infinity, manual focus

Star trails
ISO800
Aperture f8
Shutter speed 30sec minimum preferably as long as possible
Face north
Focus on infinity, manual focus

Light-painting
Focus on person doing light painting
F5.6 or higher
ISO100

Moon
Focus on moon
Aperture f8
ISO100
Shutter speed start at 1/125 and adjust from here.
You want the shutter speed to be relatively fast
as the moon is moving.

Campfires
ISO100
Focus on flames
Fill flash if want people around fire
Aperture f5.6 if just fire, f11 if people as well
Shutter speed to correct exposure
If firelight too bright wait till it burns down a bit.

Lightening
ISO 100
Focus on infinity or an object in the distance
Aperture f8 if dark, if lighting up scene f11 or
higher
Shutter speed around 4 to 30 sec